§11.

Regimental Steins of the Kaiser's Cavalry

Lieb Mädchen mein
magst ruhig sein
Mit Donner, Hagel
und Blitz schuf Gott
die Wüste Döberitz

Regimental Steins of the Kaiser's Cavalry

KÜRASSIER · DRAGOON
JÄGER ZU PFERDE · HUSSAR · UHLAN

Paul Sanders

Schiffer Military History
Atglen, PA

Acknowledgements
This book is dedicated to those who collect Imperial German Regimental Steins. During my years of collecting I have meet many individuals who share this passion. With the help of these individuals, I was able to create this book on Imperial German Cavalry Steins. I gratefully recognize the following photographer: Bob Biondi and fellow collectors who contributed: Ron Heiligenstein, Brad Sanders, Brian Sanders and Jim Turinetti.

Book design by Robert Biondi.

Library of Congress Catalog Number: 2010932033.

Printed in China.
ISBN: 978-0-7643-3683-6

Published by Schiffer Publishing Ltd.
4880 Lower Valley Road
Atglen, PA 19310
Phone: (610) 593-1777
FAX: (610) 593-2002
E-mail: Info@schifferbooks.com.
Visit our web site at: www.schifferbooks.com
Please write for a free catalog.
This book may be purchased from the publisher.
Please include $5.00 postage.
Try your bookstore first.

In Europe, Schiffer books are distributed by:
Bushwood Books
6 Marksbury Ave.
Kew Gardens, Surrey TW9 4JF
England
Phone: 44 (0)20 8392-8585
FAX: 44 (0)20 8392-9876
E-mail: info@bushwoodbooks.co.uk
www.bushwoodbooks.co.uk

Contents

KARLSRUHE-MÜHLBURG
Marktstr. 1.

Introduction

The Imperial German Cavalry consisted of 110 regiments and was divided into five separate services. There were fourteen Kurassier and heavy cavalry regiments, thirteen Jäger zu Pferde regiments, twenty-one Hussar regiments, twenty-six Uhlan regiments and thirty-six Dragoon regiments. Each of these services had their own distinct style of uniforms and headdress, along with the various colors of the uniforms themselves.

The regimental stein came into use in the late-1800s and were purchased by the servicemen to commemorate their time served. Traditionally these steins were purchased by reservist just prior to their discharge. The steins were personalized for their owner and listed in a roster format all other members of the owner's squadron.

The quality and height of the steins increased over time. Some of the difference in size depended on the depth of the pockets of the purchaser. A wealthy *Einjarigen* (one year volunteer) could buy a one liter stein while a struggling enlisted man in the same squadron would buy a standard half liter version. There were a variety of styles from the tall false bottom crockery steins to the "elegant" porcelain styles with transparent scene (lithophane) bottoms. Each stein had a pewter lid that include of German state oriented thumblift. Some had figures (finials) on the very top of the lid. Most of these figures were mounted soldiers appropriate for a cavalry unit. As World War I progressed the availability of high quality materials needed to manufacture the steins rapidly disappeared. The shortages of these goods plus the lack of skilled labor brought about and end to these works of art.

Chapter 1

Components of the Regimental Stein

Stein Body Components

Front Panel- regiment colors, leaders, insignia and uniforms

Right Side Panel – most often regiment cavalry action scenes

Left Side Panel – most often regiment cavalry romantic and village scenes

Text Inscriptions – reservist, squadron, regiment name, garrison and dates of service

Roster – list of reservists in the squadron

Handle – most crockery steins had reservist head with regimental colors on cap

Lid Components

Lid - body came in many shapes – bell, cone, and domed

Finial – figure on top of lid usual a soldier on horseback for the cavalry regiments

Thumblift – depicted the regiment's German State

Base Component

Porcelain Stein base – lithophane (semi transparent) picture within stein bottom

Crockery Stein base – large decorative flange (false bottom) adding height

Front panel showing regimental colors, uniforms, insignia, and leaders

Right side panel showing regimental home front theme

Above: Side panel showing regimental action theme

Right: Right side panel of double unit regimental showing reservist was in Ulan and Hussar regiments during his service time

Handle of Crockery stein with regimental colored service cap and Roster

Porcelain Stein Roster of names who served in the squadrons (Esk.) during the owners period of service

Top left: Lid of Bell Shape Style

Top right: Lid of Bell Shape Style with Motto

Right: Lid example of Tall Cone Style

Bottom left: Lid with Busby helmet as base of finial (rider and horse)

Bottom right: Lid of Mettlach Stein

Finial Left Side of rider on horse typical of cavalry steins

Finial Right Side rider on horse

Top left: Prussian Thumblift of Eagle with Shield

Top right: Prussian Thumblift of Broad Wing Eagle

Right: Prussian Thumblift of Swept Back Wing Eagle

Bottom left: Saxon Crest Thumblift

Bottom right: Saxon Closed Circle Crest Thumblift

Württemburg Crest Thumblift

Württemburg Sparrow with Worm Thumblift

Hessian Lion Thumblift

Bavarian Lion with Checkered Shield Thumblift

Top left: Lithophane (semi transparent pictures) in Bottom of Porcelain Regimental Steins

Top right: Lithophane Romantic Theme

Right: Lithophane Royalty Portrait Theme

Bottom left: Lithophane Homeland Theme

Bottom right: Lithophane Military Theme

Chapter 2

Regimental Stein Styles and Chronology

Porcelain Style Stein Example

Crockery/Pottery Style Stein Example

Mettlach Style Stein Examples

Mettlach Style Marked Bottom

Character Style Stein Example

Pre-1900 Early Steins were shorter
and many had hand painted panels

Standard Regimental Porcelain Stein

Post-1910 Steins tended to be taller and more ornate

Chapter 3

Prussian Heavy Cavalry - Kürassier Regiments

Regt. der Gardes du Corps,
5 Esk. Potsdam 1911 1914

Regt. der Gardes du Corps,
5 Esk. Potsdam 1911 1914 Right Panel

Regt. der Gardes du Corps,
5 Esk. Potsdam 1911 1914 Back

Regt. der Gardes du Corps,
5 Esk. Potsdam 1911 1914 Left Panel

Regt. der Gardes du Corps, Tall Crockery

Regt. der Gardes du Corps, Reservist is a Trumpeter

Regt. der Gardes du Corps, Flask

Regt. der Gardes du Corps, Flask Back Side

Regt. der Gardes du Corps and Garde-Kürass.-Regt Steins and Eagle Top Helmet

4. Esk. Garde-Kürass.-Regt. Berlin 1909-12

4. Esk. Garde-Kürass.-Regt. Berlin 1909-12 Right Side

4. Esk. Garde-Kürass.-Regt. Berlin 1909-12 Front Panel Close up

4. Esk. Garde-Kürass.-Regt. Berlin 1909-12 Back

4. Esk. Garde-Kürass.-Regt. Berlin 1909-12 Left Side

4. Esk. Garde-Kürass.-Regt. Berlin 1909-12 Pipe with Eagle Top helmet lid

LEIB-KÜR.-REGT. GROSSER KÜRFURST (SCHLES.) Nr.1

LEIB-KÜR.-REGT. GROSSER KÜRFURST (SCHLES.) Nr.1
Left Panel

LEIB-KÜR.-REGT. GROSSER KÜRFURST (SCHLES.) Nr.1
Right Panel

LEIB-KÜR.-REGT. GROSSER KÜRFURST (SCHLES.) Nr.1 Close up

LEIB-KÜR.-REGT. GROSSER KÜRFURST (SCHLES.) Nr.1 Stein with Regimental Service cap

LEIB-KÜR.-REGT. Nr.1 and KÜR.-REGT. No.2 Mettlach Steins

KÜR.-REGT. KÖNIGIN (POMM.) No2.

KÜR.-REGT. KÖNIGIN (POMM.) No2. Right Panel

KÜR.-REGT. KÖNIGIN (POMM.) No2. Left panel

KÜR.-REGT. KÖNIGIN (POMM.) No2. Back

KÜR.-REGT. KÖNIGIN (POMM.) No2. Tall Crockery

KÜR.-REGT. KÖNIGIN (POMM.) No2. Pipe Bowl

KÜR.-REGT. KÖNIGIN (POMM.) No2. Stein with Regimental Service cap and Cartridge box

KÜR.-REGT. KÖNIGIN (POMM.) No2. Bottom Mettlach Markings

There is no known example of the Kürassier Regiment Graf Wrangel (Ostpreußisches) Nr. 3 stein

Küraß.-Rgt. v. Driefen (Westfäl.) Nr.4, 4. Esk. Münster 1906 1909

Küraß.-Rgt. v. Driefen (Westfäl.) Nr.4, 4. Esk. Münster 1906 1909 Right Panel

Küraß.-Rgt. v. Driefen (Westfäl.) Nr.4, 4. Esk. Münster 1906 1909 Back

Küraß.-Rgt. v. Driefen (Westfäl.) Nr.4, 4. Esk. Münster 1906 1909 Left Panel

Küraß.-Rgt. v. Driefen (Westfäl.) Nr.4, Short (Jäger Profile) Porcelain Stein

Küraß.-Rgt. v. Driefen (Westfäl.) Nr.4, rare tall Porcelain Style

Küraß.-Rgt. v. Driefen (Westfäl.) Nr.4, Eagle Thumblift

Küraß.-Rgt. v. Driefen (Westfäl.) Nr.4, Pipe Bowl

Nr.4 and No. 5 Kürassier Regimental Steins and Kürassier Helmet

1905 4.Eskadr. Kür. Regt. Herzog Friedr. Eugen v. Württemberg Weispreuss. No.5 Riesenberg 1908

1905 4.Eskadr. Kür. Regt. Herzog Friedr. Eugen v. Württemberg Weispreuss. No.5 Riesenberg 1908 Right Side

1905 4.Eskadr. Kür. Regt. Herzog Friedr. Eugen v. Württemberg Weispreuss. No.5 Riesenberg 1908 Back

1905 4.Eskadr Kür. Regt, Herzog Friedr. Eugen v. Württemberg Weispreuss. No.5 Riesenberg 1908 Left Side

Kür. Regt. Herzog Friedr. Eugen v. Württemberg Weispreuss. No.5
Tall Crockery

Küraßier-Regt. „Kaiser Nikolaus I. v. Rußland" (Brandenb.)
Nr. 6, 1 Esk. Brandenburg 1909 1912

Küraßier-Regt. „Kaiser Nikolaus I. v. Rußland" (Brandenb.) Nr. 6, 1 Esk. Brandenburg 1909 1912 Left panel

Küraßier-Regt. „Kaiser Nikolaus I. v. Rußland" (Brandenb.) Nr. 6, 1 Esk. Brandenburg 1909 1912 Right Panel

Esk. Kür. Regt. v. Seydlitz. Magd. No 7 Halberstadt

Esk. Kür. Regt. v. Seydlitz. Magd. No 7 Halberstadt Unissued (missing esk. number and service dates)

Esk. Kür. Regt. v. Seydlitz. Magd. No 7 Halberstadt Close up

Esk. Kür. Regt. v. Seydlitz. Magd. No 7 Halberstadt Left Panel

Esk. Kür. Regt. v. Seydlitz. Magd. No 7 Halberstadt Back

Esk. Kür. Regt. v. Seydlitz. Magd. No 7 Halberstadt Glass insert top

Esk. Kür. Regt. v. Seydlitz. Magd. No 7 Halberstadt Lithophane Bottom

Kür. Regt. v. Seydlitz. Magd. No 7 Halberstadt Mettlach

Kür. Regt. v. Seydlitz. Magd. No 7 Halberstadt Pipe Bowl

Kür. Regt. v. Seydlitz. Magd. No 7 Halberstadt Steins with Service Cap

Kür. Regt. No 7 and No. 8 Steins and Helmet

4. Eskdr. Kür. Rgt. Graf Gessler Kgl No.8 Dentz 1897-1900

4. Eskdr. Kür. Rgt. Graf Gessler Kgl No.8 Dentz 1897-1900 Back

4. Eskdr. Kür. Rgt. Graf Gessler Kgl No.8 Dentz 1897-1900 Close up

4. Eskdr. Kür. Rgt. Graf Gessler Kgl No.8 Dentz 1897-1900 Right Panel

4. Eskdr. Kür. Rgt. Graf Gessler Kgl No.8 Dentz 1897-1900 Left Panel

4. Eskdr. Kür. Rgt. Graf Gessler Kgl No.8 Dentz 1897-1900 Thumblift

Kür. Rgts. No.4, 7, and 8 Pipe Bowls

Chapter 4

Saxon Heavy Cavalry Regiments

Kgl. Sächs. Garde Reiter Rgt. (1. Schweres Rgt.) 1. Esk. Dresden 1911/1914

Kgl. Sächs. Garde Reiter Rgt. (1. Schweres Rgt.) 1. Esk. Dresden 1911/1914 Right Panel

Kgl. Sächs. Garde Reiter Rgt. (1. Schweres Rgt.) 1. Esk. Dresden 1911/1914 Left Panel

Kgl. Sächs. Karabinier-Rgt.
(2. Schweres Rgt.)
3 Esk. Borna 1911 1914

Kgl. Sächs. Karabinier-Rgt.
(2. Schweres Rgt.)
3 Esk. Borna 1911 1914 Right Panel

Kgl. Sächs. Karabinier-Rgt.
(2. Schweres Rgt.)
3 Esk. Borna 1911 1914 Back

Kgl. Sächs. Karabinier-Rgt.
(2. Schweres Rgt.)
3 Esk. Borna 1911 1914
Inside Prism Top Lid

Kgl. Sächs. Karabinier-Rgt.
(2. Schweres Rgt.)
3 Esk. Borna 1911 1914
Outside Prism Top Lid

Kgl. Sächs. Karabinier-Rgt.
(2. Schweres Rgt.)
3 Esk. Borna 1911 1914 Left Panel

Chapter 5

HUSSAR REGIMENTS

Leib Esk. Leib Garde Husaren
Regiment Potsdam 1907-10

Leib Esk. Leib Garde Husaren
Regiment Potsdam 1907-10 Right Panel

Leib Esk. Leib Garde Husaren
Regiment Potsdam 1907-10 Left Panel

Leib Esk. Leib Garde Husaren
Regiment Potsdam 1907-10 Back

Leib Esk. Leib Garde Husaren Regiment Potsdam 1907-10 Lid with Finial Close up

LEIB GARDE HUSAREN REGIMENT Mettlach Style

Leib Garde Husaren Regiment Early Porcelain Style

Leib Esk. Leib Garde Husaren Regiment Potsdam 1907-10 STEIN AND NCO Busby of the regiment

1. Leib-Hus.-Rgt. Nr.1 Danzig-Langfuhr 1907-09 Front Panel

1. Leib-Hus.-Rgt. Nr.1 Danzig-Langfuhr 1907-09 Right Side Panel

1. Leib-Hus.-Rgt. Nr.1 Danzig-Langfuhr
1907-09 Back

1. Leib-Hus.-Rgt. Nr.1 Danzig-Langfuhr
1907-09 Left Side

1. Leib-Hus.-Rgt. Nr.1 Danzig-Langfuhr 1907-09 Lithophane Bottom

1. Leib-Hus.-Rgt. Nr.1 Steins and Service Cap with Regimental Skull

1. LEIB-HÜSAREN-REGT. Nr.1. Mettlach Stein Front

1. LEIB-HÜSAREN-REGT. Nr.1. Right Side

1. LEIB-HÜSAREN-REGT. Nr.1. Back

1. LEIB-HÜSAREN-REGT. Nr.1. Left Side

1. Leib-Hus.-Rgt. Nr.1 Danzig-Langfuhr 1907-09 Pipe Bowl

3 Esc. 2 Leib-Hus Reg. Königin Vict. V. Preussen No 2 Danzig-Langfuhr 1903

3 Esc. 2 Leib-Hus Reg. Königin Vict. V. Preussen No 2 Danzig-Langfuhr 1903 Right Side

3 Esc. 2 Leib-Hus Reg. Königin Vict. V. Preussen No 2 Danzig-Langfuhr 1903 Back

3 Esc. 2 Leib-Hus Reg. Königin Vict. V. Preussen No 2 Danzig-Langfuhr 1903 Left Side

3 Esc. 2 Leib-Hus Reg. Königin Vict. V. Preussen No 2 Danzig-Langfuhr 1903 Lithophane Bottom

3 Esc. 2 Leib-Hus Reg. Königin Vict. V. Preussen No 2 Danzig-Langfuhr 1903 Same Regt. Different Owner

3 Esc. 2 Leib-Hus Reg. Königin Vict. V. Preussen No 2
Danzig-Langfuhr 1903
Similar Steins with Different Flag in Front Panel

3 Esc. 2 Leib-Hus Reg. Königin Vict. V. Preussen No 2 Danzig-Langfuhr 1903 Two Owners Served Same Time

3 Esc. 2 Leib-Hus Reg. Königin Vict. V. Preussen No 2 Danzig-Langfuhr 1903 Lithophane Bottom

3 Esc. 2 Leib-Hus Reg. Königin Vict. V. Preussen No 2 Danzig-Langfuhr 1903 Steins and Officer Busby

1905 5 Esk. Hus. Rgt. V. Zieten, Brandb. No 3. In Rathenow. 1906

1905 5 Esk. Hus. Rgt. V. Zieten, Brandb. No 3. In Rathenow. 1906 Right Panel

1905 5 Esk. Hus. Rgt. V. Zieten, Brandb. No 3. In Rathenow. 1906 Back

1905 5 Esk. Hus. Rgt. V. Zieten, Brandb. No 3.
In Rathenow. 1906 Left Panel

1905 5 Esk. Hus. Rgt. V. Zieten, Brandb. No 3. In Rathenow. 1906 Apple Style Stein Bottom Panel Close up views

1905 5 Esk. Hus. Rgt. V. Zieten, Brandb. No 3. In Rathenow. 1906 Stein with Regimental Papers

HUS.-REGT. VON SCHILL (1. SCHLES.) Nr.4.

HUS.-REGT. VON SCHILL (1. SCHLES.) Nr.4. Right Side

HUS.-REGT. VON SCHILL (1. SCHLES.) Nr.4. Back

HUS.-REGT. VON SCHILL (1. SCHLES.) Nr.4. Left Side

1 Esc. Hus. Rgt. Fürst Blücher v. Wahlstatt (Pomm.) No. 5
Stolp 1903/06

1 Esc. Hus. Rgt. Fürst Blücher v. Wahlstatt (Pomm.) No. 5
Stolp 1903/06 Right Side

1 Esc. Hus. Rgt. Fürst Blücher v. Wahlstatt (Pomm.) No. 5
Stolp 1903/06 Back

1 Esc. Hus. Rgt. Fürst Blücher v. Wahlstatt (Pomm.) No. 5
Stolp 1903/06 Left Side

Hus. Rgt. Fürst Blücher v. Wahlstatt (Pomm.) No. 5 Pipe Bowl

HUS.-REGT. FÜRST BLÜCHER VON WAHLSTATT (POMM.) Nr.5.

HUS.-REGT. FÜRST BLÜCHER VON WAHLSTATT (POMM.) Nr.5. Right Side

HUS.-REGT. FÜRST BLÜCHER VON WAHLSTATT (POMM.) Nr.5. Left Side

Hus. Rgt. Fürst Blücher v. Wahlstatt (Pomm.) No. 5 Both Style Steins

Hus. Rgt. Fürst Blücher v. Wahlstatt (Pomm.) No. 5 Pipe Bowl

HUS.-REGT. GRAF GOETZEN (2. SCHLES) Nr.6. Front

HUS.-REGT. GRAF GOETZEN (2. SCHLES) Nr.6. Left Side

HUS.-REGT. GRAF GOETZEN (2. SCHLES) Nr.6. Right Side

1ST. and 2ND. SILESIAN HUSSAR REGIMENTAL STEINS

2 Esk. Husar. Regmt König Wilhem I (1 Rhein) No 7.
in Bonn 1905-1908

2 Esk. Husar. Regmt König Wilhem I (1 Rhein) No 7.
in Bonn 1905-1908 Right Front View

2 Esk. Husar. Regmt König Wilhem I (1 Rhein) No 7.
in Bonn 1905-1908 Right Side

2 Esk. Husar. Regmt König Wilhem I (1 Rhein) No 7.
in Bonn 1905-1908 Left Side and Roster

2 Esk. Husar. Regmt König Wilhem I (1 Rhein) No 7. in Bonn 1905-1908 Stein
with King Wilhelm I Cypher Shoulder Boards

2 Esk. Husar. Regmt König Wilhem I (1 Rhein) No 7. in Bonn 1905-1908
Lid with Busby Supporting Horse

4 Esk. Hus. Regt. Nic. II Rußsl. 1. Westf. No 8 Neuhaus. 1900/1903

4 Esk. Hus. Regt. Nic. II Rußsl. 1. Westf. No 8 Neuhaus. 1900/1903 Right Side

4 Esk. Hus. Regt. Nic. II Rußsl. 1. Westf. No 8 Neuhaus. 1900/1903 Back

4 Esk. Hus. Regt. Nic. II Rußsl. 1. Westf. No 8 Neuhaus. 1900/1903 Left Side

4 Esk. Hus. Regt. Nic. II Rußsl. 1. Westf. No 8 Neuhaus. 1900/1903 Lithophane Bottom

Hus. Regt. Nic. II Rußsl. 1. Westf. No 8 Neuhaus. Mettlach Plaque

4 Esk. Hus. Regt. Nic. II Rußl. 1. Westf. No 8 Neuhaus. 1900/1903 Stein with Service cap and Busby

2. Esk. Hus. Regt. Nic. II Rußsl. 1. Westf. No 8 Paderborn 1907/10 Flask

Flask Front
Close up

Flask Back

2. Esk. (2. Rhein.) Husaren Rgmt. No 9
Straßsburg l./E. 1911-1914

2. Esk. (2. Rhein.) Husaren Rgmt. No 9
Straßsburg l./E. 1911-1914 Right Side

2. Esk. (2. Rhein.) Husaren Rgmt. No 9 Straßburg l./E. 1911-1914 Front Close up

2. Esk. (2. Rhein.) Husaren Rgmt. No 9 Straßburg l./E.
1911-1914 Back and Roster

2. Esk. (2. Rhein.) Husaren Rgmt. No 9 Straßburg l./E.
1911-1914 Left Side

2. Esk. (2. Rhein.) Husaren Rgmt. No 9 Straßsburg l./E. 1911-1914 Tall Cone Style Lid

5. Esk. Magdb. Hus. Rgt. No 10 Stendal 1905/08

5. Esk. Magdb. Hus. Rgt. No 10 Stendal 1905/08 Front Close up

5. Esk. Magdb. Hus. Rgt. No 10 Stendal 1905/08 Right Side Close up

5. Esk. Magdb. Hus. Rgt. No 10 Stendal
1905/08 Right Front

5 Esk. Magdb. Hus. Rgt. No 10 Stendal
1905/08 Back

5. Esk. Magdb. Hus. Rgt. No 10 Stendal 1905/08 Right Side

5. Esk. Magdb. Hus. Rgt. No 10 Stendal 1905/08 Left Panel

MAGDEB. HUSAREN-REGT. No. 10. Mettlach Style Stein

Magdb. Hus. Rgt. No 10 Pipe

5. Esk. Magdb. Hus. Rgt. No 10 Stendal 1905/08
Stein and NCO Parade Busby

5 Esk. 2. Westf. Husaren Regiment N: 11 Crefeld 1908/1911

5 Esk. 2. Westf. Husaren Regiment N: 11 Crefeld 1908/1911 Right Side

5 Esk. 2. Westf. Husaren Regiment N: 11
Crefeld 1908/1911 Back

2. Westf. Husaren Regiment N: 11 Crockery Stein
with Unique Regimental Uniform and Pennant Colors

5 Esk. 2. Westf. Husaren Regiment N: 11 Crefeld 1908/1911
Left Side and Regt. Sabretache

5 Esk. 2. Westf. Husaren Regiment N: 11 Crefeld 1908/1911
Steins and Sabretache

4 Eskr Thüring. Hus. Regt. No12.
Torgau. 1908.11.

4 Eskr Thüring. Hus. Regt. No12.
Torgau. 1908.11. Back

4 Eskr Thüring. Hus. Regt. No12. Torgau. 1908.11. Front Close up

4 Eskr Thüring. Hus. Regt. No12.
Torgau. 1908.11. Right Side

4 Eskr Thüring. Hus. Regt. No12.
Torgau. 1908.11. Left Side

4 Eskr Thüring. Hus. Regt. No12. Torgau. 1908.11
Stein and Service Cap

4 Eskdr. Hus. Rgt. König Humb. V. Italien 1. Kürhess. No 13 Diedenhofen 1906-09
Stein with Busby

4 Eskdr. Hus. Rgt. König Humb. V. Italien 1. Kürhess. No 13 Diedenhofen 1906-09 Front Panel

4 Eskdr. Hus. Rgt. König Humb. V. Italien 1. Kürhess. No 13 Diedenhofen 1906-09 Right Panel

4 Eskdr. Hus. Rgt. König Humb. V. Italien 1. Kürhess. No 13 Diedenhofen 1906-09 Close up

4 Eskdr. Hus. Rgt. König Humb. V. Italien 1. Kürhess. No 13 Diedenhofen 1906-09 Back showing it is a full 1 Liter stein

4 Eskdr. Hus. Rgt. König Humb. V. Italien 1. Kürhess. No 13 Diedenhofen 1906-09 Left Panel

4 Eskdr. Hus. Rgt. König Humb. V. Italien 1. Kürhess. No 13 Diedenhofen 1906-09
Stein with King Umberto Cypher Shoulder Board

5 Esk. Hus. Regt.Landgraf Friedr. II. v. Hessen Homburg
(2. Kurhess.) Nro.14 Cassel 1911-14

5 Esk. Hus. Regt.Landgraf Friedr. II. v. Hessen Homburg
(2. Kurhess.) Nro.14 Cassel 1911-14 Back

5 Esk. Hus. Regt.Landgraf Friedr. II. v. Hessen Homburg (2. Kurhess.) Nro.14 Cassel 1911-14 Close up

5 Esk. Hus. Regt.Landgraf Friedr. II. v. Hessen Homburg (2. Kurhess.) Nro.14 Cassel 1911-14 Right Side

5 Esk. Hus. Regt.Landgraf Friedr. II. v. Hessen Homburg (2. Kurhess.) Nro.14 Cassel 1911-14 Left Side

4 Esk. Hus. Regt. Königin Wilhelmina d. Niederl. Hannov. No 15 Wandsbek 1907-10

4 Esk. Hus. Regt. Königin Wilhelmina d. Niederl. Hannov. No 15 Wandsbek 1907-10 Back

4 Esk. Hus. Regt. Königin Wilhelmina d. Niederl. Hannov. No 15 Wandsbek 1907-10 Right Side

4 Esk. Hus. Regt. Königin Wilhelmina d. Niederl. Hannov. No 15 Wandsbek 1907-10 Left Side

4 Esk. Hus. Regt. Königin Wilhelmina d. Niederl.
Hannov. No 15 Wandsbek 1907-10
Stein, Busby and Queen Wilhelmina Cypher Shoulder Board

4 Esk. Hus. Rgt. Kaiser Franz Josef v. Ostereich (Schlesw. Hollst.) Nr 16 Schleswig 1910-13

4 Esk. Hus. Rgt. Kaiser Franz Josef v. Ostereich (Schlesw. Hollst.) Nr 16 Schleswig 1910-13 Back

4 Esk. Hus. Rgt. Kaiser Franz Josef v. Ostereich (Schlesw. Hollst.) Nr 16 Schleswig 1910-13 Close up

4 Esk. Hus. Rgt. Kaiser Franz Josef v. Ostereich (Schlesw. Hollst.) Nr 16 Schleswig 1910-13 Right Side

4 Esk. Hus. Rgt. Kaiser Franz Josef v. Ostereich (Schlesw. Hollst.) Nr 16 Schleswig 1910-13 Left Side

4 Esk. Hus. Rgt. Kaiser Franz Josef v. Ostereich (Schlesw. Hollst.) Nr 16 Schleswig 1910-13
Stein with Kaiser Franz Josef Cypher Shoulder Boards

4 Esk 1899 Braunschw. Hus. Rgt. N:17 Braunschweig. 1902

4 Esk 1899 Braunschw. Hus. Rgt. N:17 Braunschweig. 1902 Back

4 Esk 1899 Braunschw. Hus. Rgt. N:17 Braunschweig. 1902 Close up of Regimental Skull and Sabretache

4 Esk 1899 Braunschw. Hus. Rgt. N:17 Braunschweig. 1902 Right Side

4 Esk 1899 Braunschw. Hus. Rgt. N:17 Braunschweig. 1902 Left Side

4 Esk 1899 Braunschw. Hus. Rgt. N:17 Braunschweig. 1902 Lithophane Bottom

4 Esk 1899 Braunschw. Hus. Rgt. N:17 Braunschweig. 1902 Close up of Regt. Battle Honors

Braunschw. Hus. Rgt. N:17 Stein, Service Cap and Busby

Braunschw. Hus. Rgt. N:17 Commemorative Ash Tray

Braunschw. Hus. Rgt. N:17 Commemorative Ash Tray Inside Markings

2. Eskd. Braunschw. Hus Rgt N. 17 in Braunschweig 1908/11 Character Style Skull Stein

2. Eskd. Braunschw. Hus Rgt N. 17 in Braunschweig 1908/11 Stein showing unique Regimental Inscription location on Lid

3. Esk. Braunschw. Hus Rgt N. 17 in Braunschweig 1909 Original Photo of Hussars using steins

2. Eskd. Braunschw. Hus Rgt N. 17
in Braunschweig 1908/11
Side view with Finial horse and rider

BRAUNSCHW. HUSAREN-REGT. No. 17. Mettlach Style Stein

Braunschw. Hus. Rgt. N:17 Pipe Bowl

1.Husar Rgt. „ König Albert" Nr.18, Großenhain 1910 1913

1.Husar Rgt. „ König Albert" Nr.18, Großenhain 1910 1913 Back

1.Husar Rgt. „ König Albert" Nr.18, Großenhain 1910 1913 Close up

1.Husar Rgt. „ König Albert" Nr.18, Großenhain 1910 1913 Right Side

1.Husar Rgt. „ König Albert" Nr.18, Großenhain 1910 1913 Left Side

1.Husar Rgt. „ König Albert“ Nr.18, Großenhain 1910 1913
Showing Screw Off Lid

1.Husar Rgt. „ König Albert“ Nr.18, Großenhain 1910 1913 Stein
showing lid insert of King Albert of Saxony

3. Eskr. 2 Kgl. Sächs. Hus. Rgt. Königin Carola Nr.19.
Grimma 1910-13

3. Eskr. 2 Kgl. Sächs. Hus. Rgt. Königin Carola Nr.19.
Grimma 1910-13 Back

3. Eskr. 2 Kgl. Sächs. Hus. Rgt. Königin Carola Nr.19. Grimma 1910-13 Right Side

3. Eskr. 2 Kgl. Sächs. Hus. Rgt. Königin Carola Nr.19. Grimma 1910-13 Left Side

3. Eskr. 2 Kgl. Sächs. Hus. Rgt. Königin Carola Nr.19. Stein and Busby

Kgl. Sächs. 3. Husaren-Regt. 20, 3 Esk. Bautzen. 1909-12

Kgl. Sächs. 3. Husaren-Regt. 20, 3 Esk. Bautzen. 1909-12 Back

Kgl. Sächs. 3. Husaren-Regt. 20, 3 Esk. Bautzen. 1909-12 Right Side

Kgl. Sächs. 3. Husaren-Regt. 20, 3 Esk. Bautzen. 1909-12 Left Side

Kgl. Sächs. 3. Husaren-Regt. 20, 3 Esk. Bautzen. 1909-12
Right side showing double regimental 17th Ulan service time

Kgl. Sächs. 3. Husaren-Regt. 20, 3 Esk. Bautzen. 1909-12
Left Side showing 20th Hussar service time

Kgl. Sächs. 3. Husaren-Regt. 20, 3 Esk. Bautzen. 1909-12
Lithophane Bottom

All Three Saxon Regiments in Porcelain style steins

4 Eskr. 3. Kgl. Sächs. Husaren Regt. 20 Bautzen. 1909-12

4 Eskr. 3. Kgl. Sächs. Husaren Regt. 20 Bautzen. 1909-12 Back

4 Eskr. 3. Kgl. Sächs. Husaren Regt. 20 Bautzen. 1909-12 Right Side

4 Eskr. 3. Kgl. Sächs. Husaren Regt. 20 Bautzen. 1909-12 Left Side

4 Eskr. 3. Kgl. Sächs. Husaren Regt. 20 Bautzen. 1909-12
Left Side showing double regiments of Hussar and Ulan

4 Eskr. 3. Kgl. Sächs. Husaren Regt. 20 Bautzen. 1909-12
Right Panels showing double regiments of Hussar and Ulan

3. Kgl. Sächs. Husaren Regt. 20 Steins and Service cap

Chapter 6

Uhlan Regiments

1. Esc. 1tes Garde Ulanen regim. Potsdam 1912-1915.

1. Esc. 1tes Garde Ulanen regim. Potsdam 1912-1915. Back

1. Esc. 1tes Garde Ulanen regim. Potsdam 1912-1915. Right Side

1. Esc. 1tes Garde Ulanen regim. Potsdam 1912-1915. Left Side

1tes Garde Ulanen regim. Tall 1 Liter Crockery Stein

2 Garde Ulan Regt. Berlin 1903-1906

2 Garde Ulan Regt. Berlin 1903-1906 Back

2 Garde Ulan Regt. Berlin 1903-1906 Right Side

2 Garde Ulan Regt. Berlin 1903-1906 Left Side

5 Esc. 3rd Garde Ulanen regt. Potsdam 1903-1906

5 Esc. 3rd Garde Ulanen regt. Potsdam 1903-1906 Back

5 Esc. 3rd Garde Ulanen regt. Potsdam 1903-1906 Right Side

5 Esc. 3rd Garde Ulanen regt. Potsdam 1903-1906 Left Side

Lithophane Bottom with picture of The Kaiser

5 Esc. Ulan regt. Kaiser Alexander III. v. Rußland Westpruß. No 1 Militsch 1901-1904

5 Esc. Ulan regt. Kaiser Alexander III. v. Rußland Westpruß. No 1 Militsch 1901-1904 Back

Lithophane Bottom

5 Esc. Ulan regt. Kaiser Alexander III. v. Rußland Westpruß. No 1 Militsch 1901-1904 Right Panel

5 Esc. Ulan regt. Kaiser Alexander III. v. Rußland Westpruß. No 1 Militsch 1901-1904 Left Panel

3 Esk. Ulan Rgt. V. Katzler Schles No. 2
Gleiwitz 1904-1909

3 Esk. Ulan Rgt. V. Katzler Schles No. 2
Gleiwitz 1904-1909 Back

*3 Esk. Ulan Rgt. V. Katzler Schles No. 2
Gleiwitz 1904-1909 Right Side*

*3 Esk. Ulan Rgt. V. Katzler Schles No. 2
Gleiwitz 1904-1909 Left Side*

2 Esc. Ulan Reg. Kais. Alex. II (1 Brdb) No. 3
Fürstenwalde 1910-1913

2 Esc. Ulan Reg. Kais. Alex. II (1 Brdb) No. 3
Fürstenwalde 1910-1913 Back

2 Esc. Ulan Reg. Kais. Alex. II (1 Brdb) No. 3 Fürstenwalde 1910-1913
Close up of Epaulette on Thumblift

2 Esc. Ulan Reg. Kais. Alex. II (1 Brdb) No. 3
Fürstenwalde 1910-1913 Right Side

2 Esc. Ulan Reg. Kais. Alex. II (1 Brdb) No. 3
Fürstenwalde 1910-1913 Left Side

1 Eskadr. Ulanen Regt. v. Schmidt 1. Pomm. No.4
Thorn 1909-1912

1 Eskadr. Ulanen Regt. v. Schmidt 1. Pomm. No.4
Thorn 1909-1912 Back

1 Eskadr. Ulanen Regt. v. Schmidt 1. Pomm. No.4
Thorn 1909-1912 Right Panel

1 Eskadr. Ulanen Regt. v. Schmidt 1. Pomm. No.4
Thorn 1909-1912 Left Panel

4 Esc. Westfälisches Ulanen Regiment No. 5
Düsseldorf 1904-07

4 Esc. Westfälisches Ulanen Regiment No. 5
Düsseldorf 1904-07 Back

4 Esc. Westfälisches Ulanen Regiment No. 5
Düsseldorf 1904-07 Right Side

4 Esc. Westfälisches Ulanen Regiment No. 5
Düsseldorf 1904-07 Left Side

1 Esk. Ulan Rgt. König Christian IX Dänemark Thür. No 6 Hanau 1910-13

1 Esk. Ulan Rgt. König Christian IX Dänemark Thür. No 6 Hanau 1910-13 Back

1 Esk. Ulan Rgt. König Christian IX Dänemark Thür. No 6 Hanau 1910-13 Right Side

1 Esk. Ulan Rgt. König Christian IX Dänemark Thür. No 6 Hanau 1910-13 Left Side

Ulan Rgt. König Christian IX Dänemark Thür. No 6 Hanau Pipe Bowl

4 Esk. Ulanen Rgt. Grossh. Friedr. V. Baden Rhein. No.7
Saarbrücken 1906-1907

4 Esk. Ulanen Rgt. Grossh. Friedr. V. Baden Rhein. No.7
Saarbrücken 1906-1907 Back

4 Esk. Ulanen Rgt. Grossh. Friedr. V. Baden Rhein. No.7 Saarbrücken 1906-1907 Right Panel

4 Esk. Ulanen Rgt. Grossh. Friedr. V. Baden Rhein. No.7 Saarbrücken 1906-1907 Left Panel

ULAN. REGT. GRAF ZU DOHNA (OSTPR.) No. 8

ULAN. REGT. GRAF ZU DOHNA (OSTPR.) No. 8 Back

ULAN. REGT. GRAF ZU DOHNA (OSTPR.) No. 8 Left Side

ULAN. REGT. GRAF ZU DOHNA (OSTPR.) No. 8 Right Side

2 Esk. (2. Pomm.) Ulan Rgt. No. 9
Demmin 1899-1901

2 Esk. (2. Pomm.) Ulan Rgt. No. 9
Demmin 1899-1901 Back

2 Esk. (2. Pomm.) Ulan Rgt. No. 9 Demmin 1899-1901 Right Side

2 Esk. (2. Pomm.) Ulan Rgt. No. 9 Demmin 1899-1901 Left Side

ULAN.-REGT. PRINZ AUGUST VON WÜRTTEMBERG (POSEN) Nr 10

ULAN.-REGT. PRINZ AUGUST VON WÜRTTEMBERG (POSEN) Nr 10 Back

ULAN.-REGT. PRINZ AUGUST VON WÜRTTEMBERG (POSEN) Nr 10
Right Side

ULAN.-REGT. PRINZ AUGUST VON WÜRTTEMBERG (POSEN) Nr 10
Left Side

Ulan.-Regt. Prinz August Von Württemberg (Posen) Nr 10 Flask

Ulan.-Regt. Prinz August Von Württemberg (Posen) Nr 10 Flask Back

3 Esk. 2. Brandenb. Ulan Rgmt. Nr 11
Saarburg Jahr 1909-12

3 Esk. 2. Brandenb. Ulan Rgmt. Nr 11
Saarburg Jahr 1909-12 Back

3 Esk. 2. Brandenb. Ulan Rgmt. Nr 11
Saarburg Jahr 1909-12 Right Side

3 Esk. 2. Brandenb. Ulan Rgmt. Nr 11
Saarburg Jahr 1909-12 Left Side

LITTH. ULAN.-REGT. Nr 12.

LITTH. ULAN.-REGT. Nr 12. Back

LITTH. ULAN.-REGT. Nr 12. Right Side

LITTH. ULAN.-REGT. Nr 12. Left Side

2 Esc. König Ulan Regt. (1 Hanov.) No. 13
Hannover 1906-10

2 Esc. König Ulan Regt. (1 Hanov.) No. 13
Hannover 1906-10 Back

2 Esc. König Ulan Regt. (1 Hanov.) No. 13
Hannover 1906-10 Right Side

2 Esc. König Ulan Regt. (1 Hanov.) No. 13
Hannover 1906-10 Left Side

König Ulan Regt. (1 Hanov.) No. 13
Officer Helmet with Regimental Battle Honors on Front Plate

1 Esk. Ulan Rgt. Groz Frans v. Ostreich 2
Hann. No. 14 St.Avold 1896-99

1 Esk. Ulan Rgt. Groz Frans v. Ostreich 2
Hann. No. 14 St.Avold 1896-99 Back

1 Esk. Ulan Rgt. Groz Frans v. Ostreich 2 Hann. No. 14 St.Avold 1896-99 Right Panel

1 Esk. Ulan Rgt. Groz Frans v. Ostreich 2 Hann. No. 14 St.Avold 1896-99 Left Panel

1 Esk. Ulan Rgt. Groz Frans v. Ostreich 2 Hann. No. 14 St.Avold 1896-99 Lithophane Bottom

Ulan Rgt. Groz Frans v. Ostreich 2 Hann. No. 14 Officer Helmet with Parade Bush

5 Esc. Schlesw. Hosst. Ulanen Regt. No. 15
Saarburg 1907-10

5 Esc. Schlesw. Hosst. Ulanen Regt. No. 15
Saarburg 1907-10 Back

5 Esc. Schlesw. Hosst. Ulanen Regt. No. 15 Saarburg 1907-10 Right Side

5 Esc. Schlesw. Hosst. Ulanen Regt. No. 15 Saarburg 1907-10 Left Side

3 Esc. Ulan Regt. No. 16 Hennigs v. Treffenfeld
Altmark Garde Legen 1897-1900

3 Esc. Ulan Regt. No. 16 Hennigs v. Treffenfeld
Altmark Garde Legen 1897-1900 Back

3 Esc. Ulan Regt. No. 16 Hennigs v. Treffenfeld Altmark Garde Legen 1897-1900 Lithophane Bottom

3 Esc. Ulan Regt. No. 16 Hennigs v. Treffenfeld Altmark Garde Legen 1897-1900 Right Side

3 Esc. Ulan Regt. No. 16 Hennigs v. Treffenfeld Altmark Garde Legen 1897-1900 Left Side

4 Esk. 1. Kgl. Sächs. Ulan Rgt. No.17 Kaiser Frz. Jos. V. Oesterr. König V. Ungarn Oschatz 1906-09

4 Esk. 1. Kgl. Sächs. Ulan Rgt. No.17 Kaiser Frz. Jos. V. Oesterr. König V. Ungarn Oschatz 1906-09 Back

4 Esk. 1. Kgl. Sächs. Ulan Rgt. No.17 Kaiser Frz. Jos. V. Oesterr. König V. Ungarn Oschatz 1906-09 Right View

4 Esk. 1. Kgl. Sächs. Ulan Rgt. No.17 Kaiser Frz. Jos. V. Oesterr. König V. Ungarn Oschatz 1906-09 Left View

1.Esk. 2. Kgl. Sächs. Ulan Regt. No. 18. Leipzig. 1901-04

1.Esk. 2. Kgl. Sächs. Ulan Regt. No. 18. Leipzig. 1901-04 Back

1.Esk. 2. Kgl. Sächs. Ulan Regt. No. 18. Leipzig. 1901-04 Right Side

1.Esk. 2. Kgl. Sächs. Ulan Regt. No. 18. Leipzig. 1901-04 Left Side

Ulan.-Regt. König Karl (Württ.) Nr.19 Ulm 4 Esk. 1906/09

Ulan.-Regt. König Karl (Württ.) Nr.19 Ulm 4 Esk. 1906/09 Back

Ulan.-Regt. König Karl (Württ.) Nr.19 Ulm 4 Esk. 1906/09 Right Side

Ulan.-Regt. König Karl (Württ.) Nr.19 Ulm 4 Esk. 1906/09 Left Side

3. Esk. Ulan Regt. König Wilhl. 2. Württ. No 20.
Ludwigsburg.1909-12

3. Esk. Ulan Regt. König Wilhl. 2. Württ. No 20.
Ludwigsburg.1909-12 Back

3. Esk. Ulan Regt. König Wilhl. 2. Württ. No 20. Ludwigsburg. 1909-12 Right Panel

3. Esk. Ulan Regt. König Wilhl. 2. Württ. No 20. Ludwigsburg. 1909-12 Left Panel

Ulan Regt. König Wilhl. 2. Württ. No 20. Officer Helmet

Kgl. Sächs. 3 Ulanen-Rgt. Nr. 21 Kaiser Wilhelm II., König v. Preussen 1Esk. Chemnitz 1905/08

Kgl. Sächs. 3 Ulanen-Rgt. Nr. 21 Kaiser Wilhelm II., König v. Preussen 1Esk. Chemnitz 1905/08 Back

Kgl. Sächs. 3 Ulanen-Rgt. Nr. 21 Kaiser Wilhelm II., König v. Preussen 1Esk. Chemnitz 1905/08 Right Panel

Kgl. Sächs. 3 Ulanen-Rgt. Nr. 21 Kaiser Wilhelm II., König v. Preussen 1Esk. Chemnitz 1905/08 Left Panel

Kgl. Sächs. 3 Ulanen-Rgt. Nr. 21 Officers Parade Helmet

Kgl. Bay. 1. Ulan Regt. Kaiser Wilh II. 4. Esk.
Bamb. 1905/08

Kgl. Bay. 1. Ulan Regt. Kaiser Wilh II. 4. Esk.
Bamb. 1905/08 Back

Kgl. Bay. 1. Ulan Regt. Kaiser Wilh II. 4. Esk. Bamb. 1905/08 Right Panel

Kgl. Bay. 1. Ulan Regt. Kaiser Wilh II. 4. Esk. Bamb. 1905/08 Left Panel

Kgl. Bay. 1. Ulan Regt. Kaiser Wilh II. 4. Esk. Bamb. 1905/08
Lithophane Bottom of King Ludwig

Kgl. Bay. 1. Ulan Regt. Kaiser Wilh II. Bamb. Pipe Bowl

Kgl. Bay. 2. Ulanen Regt. König 5. Esk 1907/10 Ansbach

Kgl. Bay. 2. Ulanen Regt. König 5. Esk 1907/10 Ansbach Back

Kgl. Bay. 2. Ulanen Regt. König 5. Esk 1907/10 Ansbach Right Side

Kgl. Bay. 2. Ulanen Regt. König 5. Esk 1907/10 Ansbach Left Side

Chapter 7

Representative Jäger zu Pferde (JZP) (Mounted Riflemen) Regiments

2. Esk. Jäger zu Pferde No. 2 Langensalza 1908-11

4. Esk. Jäger zu Pferde Nro. 3 Colmar 1911-14.

4. Esk. Jäger zu Pferde Nro. 3 Colmar 1911-14. Back

4. Esk. Jäger zu Pferde Nro. 3 Colmar 1911-14.Close up

4. Esk. Jäger zu Pferde Nro. 3 Colmar 1911-14.
Right Side of 1 Liter Porcelain Style stein

4. Esk. Jäger zu Pferde
Nro. 3 Colmar 1911-14.
Lithophane Bottom

4. Esk. Jäger zu Pferde Nro. 3 Colmar 1911-14. Left Side

2. Esk. Jäger z. Pferde Nr. 5 Mülhausen E. 1911-14

Chapter 8

Representative Dragoon Regiments

5. Esk. Hagdeb. Drag. Regt. No 6 Diedenbofen. 94-97

5. Esk. Hagdeb. Drag. Regt. No 6 Diedenbofen. 94-97 Back

5. Esk. Hagdeb. Drag. Regt. No 6 Diedenbofen. 94-97 Right Side

5. Esk. Hagdeb. Drag. Regt. No 6 Diedenbofen. 94-97 Left Side

2. GROSSH. MECKLENB. DRAGONER-REGT. Nr. 18 Mettlach Style

2. GROSSH. MECKLENB. DRAGONER-REGT. Nr. 18 Back

2. GROSSH. MECKLENB. DRAGONER-REGT. Nr. 18 Right Side

2. GROSSH. MECKLENB. DRAGONER-REGT. Nr. 18 Left Side

Mecklenburg Dragoon 18th Stein and Helmet

3.Esk. Garde Drag. Regiment 1. Grolsh. Hess. No 23
Darmstadt 1908.11.

3.Esk. Garde Drag. Regiment 1. Grolsh. Hess. No 23
Darmstadt 1908.11. Back

3.Esk. Garde Drag. Regiment 1. Grolsh. Hess. No 23 Darmstadt 1908.11. Lithophane Bottom

3.Esk. Garde Drag. Regiment 1. Grolsh. Hess. No 23 Darmstadt 1908.11. Right Side

3.Esk. Garde Drag. Regiment 1. Grolsh. Hess. No 23 Darmstadt 1908.11. Left Side

Hessian Dragoon 23rd Stein, Officer Helmet and 24th Hessian Dragoon Stein

2. Esk. Leib Drag. Regt. Kais. Nicol. II. v. Rußl. 2. Großh. Hess. Nr 24. Darmstadt. 1910-13

2. Esk. Leib Drag. Regt. Kais. Nicol. II. v. Rußl. 2. Großh. Hess. Nr 24. Darmstadt. 1910-13 Back

2. Esk. Leib Drag. Regt. Kais. Nicol. II. v. Rußl. 2. Großh. Hess. Nr 24. Darmstadt. 1910-13 Right Side

2. Esk. Leib Drag. Regt. Kais. Nicol. II. v. Rußl. 2. Großh. Hess. Nr 24. Darmstadt. 1910-13 Left Side

§11.